Essential Audition Songs for

KiDS

© International Music Publications Ltd
First published in 2000 by International Music Publications Ltd
International Music Publications Ltd is a Faber Music company
Bloomsbury House 74–77 Great Russell Street London WC1B 3DA
Series Editor: Sadie Cook
Editorial, production and recording: Artemis Music Limited
Design and Production: Space DPS Limited
Printed in England by Caligraving Ltd
All rights reserved

ISBN10: 0-571-52680-2
EAN13: 978-0-571-52680-2

To buy Faber Music publications or to find out about the full range of titles available,
please contact your local music retailer or Faber Music sales enquiries:

Faber Music Ltd, Burnt Mill, Elizabeth Way, Harlow, CM20 2HX England
Tel: +44(0)1279 82 89 82   Fax: +44(0)1279 82 89 83
sales@fabermusic.com   fabermusic.com

FABER *ff* MUSIC

In the book

On the CD

Bugsy Malone

(from *Bugsy Malone*)

Words and Music by Paul Williams

Consider Yourself

(from *Oliver*)

Words and Music by Lionel Bart

Moderate march tempo

Con - sid - er your - self____ at home,____
sid - er your - self____ well in:____

____ con - sid - er your - self____ one of the
____ con - sid - er your - self____ part of the

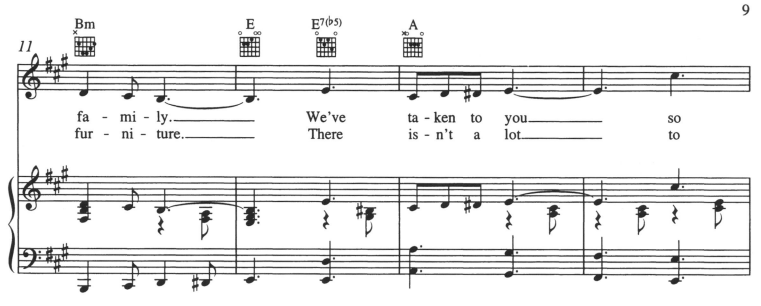

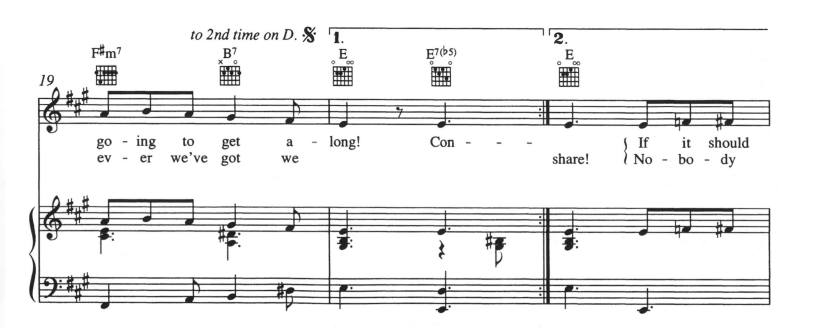

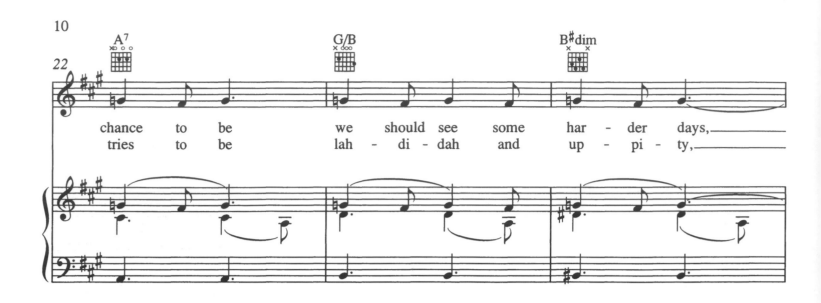

chance to be we should see some har - der days,_____
tries to be lah - di - dah and up - pi - ty,_____

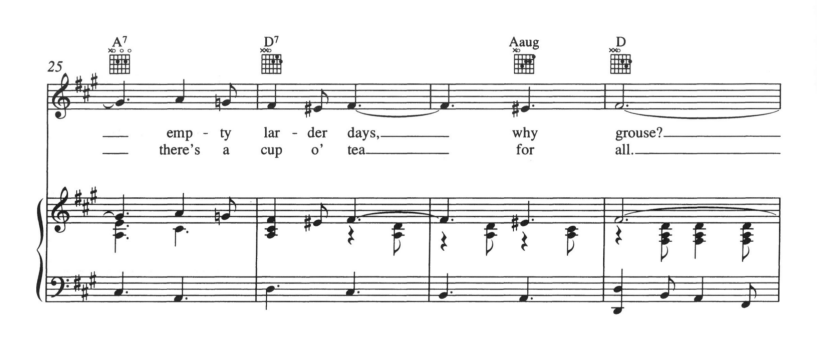

_____ emp - ty lar - der days,_____ why grouse?_____
_____ there's a cup o' tea_____ for all._____

_____ Al - ways a chance we'll meet some - bo - dy to
_____ On - ly it's wise to be han - dy wiv a

My Favorite Things

(from *The Sound of Music*)

Lyrics by Oscar Hammerstein II
Music by Richard Rodgers

Love's Got A Hold On My Heart

Words and Music by
Andrew Frampton and Pete Waterman

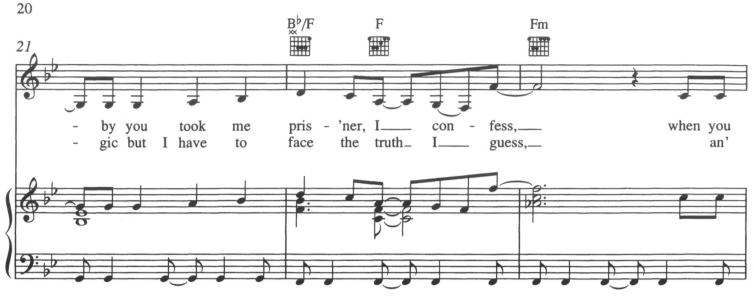

- by you took me pris - 'ner, I___ con - fess,___ when you

- gic but I have to face the truth___ I___ guess, an'

crossed my de - fen - ces and cap - - tured my heart. An' now it's too late

live ev - er - more___ re - signed___ to my fate. 'Cos now it's too late___

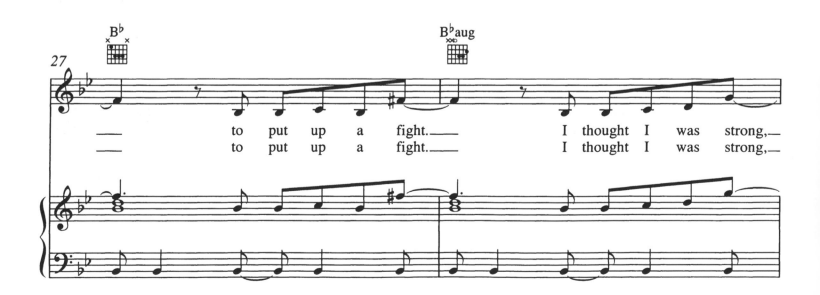

___ to put up a fight.___ I thought I was strong,___

___ to put up a fight.___ I thought I was strong,___

Maybe This Time

(from *Cabaret*)

Words by Fred Ebb
Music by John Kander

Slowly

May-be this time I'll be luc - ky.—

May-be this time— he'll stay. May - be this time,—

My Name Is Tallulah

(from *Bugsy Malone*)

Words and Music by Paul Williams

try to leave a lit-tle re-pu-ta-tion be-hind_ me   so if you real-ly need to, you'll

know how to find_ me.

My name is Tal-lu-lah,   I

live till I die,_   I'll take what you give_ me and I won't ask why._   I've

o - pen in - vi - ta - tion is the road I'll tra - vel on. I'll

ne - ver say good - bye be - cause the words up - set___ me. You

may for - give my go - ing but you won't for - get___ me.

D. %: al Coda

CODA

Tal - lu - lah.___

Over The Rainbow

(from *The Wizard of Oz*)

Words by E Y Harburg
Music by Harold Arlen

When all the world is a hope-less jum-ble, and the rain-drops tum-ble all a-round, hea-ven o-pens a ma-gic lane.

When all the clouds dark-en up the sky-way, there's a

You're Never Fully Dressed
Without A Smile

(from *Annie*)

Words by Martin Charnin
Music by Charles Strouse

We're In The Money

(from *42nd Street*)

Words by Al Dubin
Music by Harry Warren

46

Wouldn't It Be Loverly

(from *My Fair Lady*)

Words by Alan Jay Lerner
Music by Frederick Loewe

who takes good care of me. Oh would – – n't

it be lov - er - ly?

Lov - er - ly!

Lov - er - ly! Lov - er - ly! Lov - er - ly!

ESSENTIAL AUDITION SONGS

KIDS	**Kids**	MALE	**Broadway**
FEMALE	**Broadway**	MALE	**Pop Ballads**
FEMALE	**Jazz Standards**	MALE	**Timeless Crooners**
FEMALE	**Movie Hits**	MALE & FEMALE	**Comedy Songs**
FEMALE	**Pop Ballads**	MALE & FEMALE	**Duets**
FEMALE	**Pop Divas**	MALE & FEMALE	**Wannabe Pop Stars**
FEMALE	**West End Hits**	MALE & FEMALE	**Love Songs**

FABER _ff_ MUSIC

To buy Faber Music publications or to find out about the full range of titles available
please contact your local music retailer or Faber Music sales enquiries:

Faber Music Ltd, Burnt Mill, Elizabeth Way, Harlow CM20 2HX
Tel: +44 (0) 1279 82 89 82   Fax: +44 (0) 1279 82 89 83
sales@fabermusic.com   fabermusic.com   expressprintmusic.com